T0380971

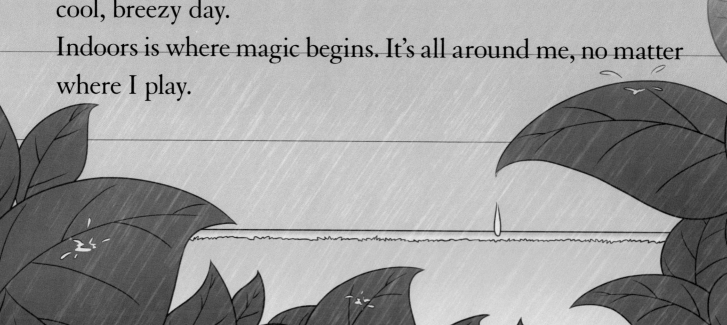

The morning has finally come.

I eagerly want to share with you the magic within our surrounds.

I hear the tapping of rain on my bedroom window; it's a cool, breezy day.

Indoors is where magic begins. It's all around me, no matter where I play.

I use my eyes to see and explore my surrounds.
My mind's imagination is also a part of my playground.
I feel the stir of magic move from deep within.
It feels like colors glowing and sparkling and beginning to spin.

A sense of wonder is allowing new dreams to spring about.

My abundant magic is being revealed, mesmerizing and spellbinding.

I'm dreaming up a new idea in this thinking and feeling process.

So much fun is revealing a path that is always freely accessed.

I want to paint this magical dream to show you what I am feeling,

Bringing to life what caught my excitement and wonder, its soul and heart appealing.

Going to use as many colors imaginable to stroke with a paintbrush.

The spectacular magic of color will soon start flowing out in a rush.

Everything is ready now; I'm beginning something new.
With my focused leap of faith, attention to detail will be used all the way through.
Red, orange, and yellow powerfully begin to light up the picture.
Imagining the flickering of fire helps me remember the color mixture.

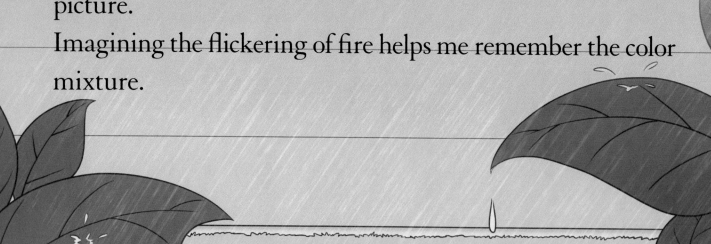

Green and blue are beautiful together when painted by each other's side.
I'm drawn to look outside my window; it's no longer raining, and wind has subsided.

Peering and shining through now is the sun, lighting the way,
Revealing a bright blue sky and the glistening green grass,
which was washed by the rain.

The deep warmth of indigo and violet are the colors I will paint with next.

They remind me of the night sky with the moon glowing and reflecting against it.

My painting is special and unique to me, and I was able to bring it to life.

The colors all feel like magical threads made up of energetic light.

I am outside now to hang my painting over the branch of a tree.
The colors stand out as it sways in the cool wind, drying carefully.
Something in the corner of my eye has now taken my gaze.
The blaze from one end of the sky to the other are of a rainbow's rays.

Just like my painting, I see the colors red, orange, and yellow. The rainbow is spotted by clouds that resemble fluffy marshmallows.

Green, blue, indigo, and violet are also colors displayed right across the sky.

Beautifully balanced all together, united and shared with all for the public eye.

So much magic is revealed today, starting with imagination and belief.

Next was movement of the paintbrush that flicked the paper with relief.

My painted rainbow matches the one outdoors; this has been a unique treat.

Its synchronicity is the magic that makes this journey wonderfully complete.

Copyright © 2019 by Veronica Red. 780368

ISBN: Softcover   978-1-7960-0026-9
        EBook   978-1-7960-0025-2

All rights reserved. No part of this book may
be reproduced or transmitted in any form or by
any means, electronic or mechanical, including
photocopying, recording, or by any information storage
and retrieval system, without permission in writing from
the copyright owner.

Print information available on the last page

Rev. date: 01/23/2019

To order additional copies of this book, contact:
Xlibris
1-888-795-4274
www.Xlibris.com
Orders@Xlibris.com

Printed in the United States
By Bookmasters